WAITING FOR SUNSET TO BURY RED CAMELLIAS

POEMS BY
MIHO KINNAS

FREE VERSE PRESS
A FREE VERSE, LLC EXPERIENCE

The author is available for performances. If interested, please email **miho.kinnas@gmail.com**

ISBN: 9798987163290

Library of Congress Control Number: 2023947735

Layout and design by Marcus Amaker
Author photo by Lyndsi Caulder

Printed in the United States of America.
First printing edition 2023.

Published by Free Verse Press
Free Verse, LLC
North Charleston, South Carolina
freeversepress.com

感謝を込めて本書は詩人の田中郁子氏に捧げます。

I dedicate this book to a poet, Ikuko Tanaka (October 2, 1937 - August 6, 2021) along with the fond memory of cooking together in her mother's kitchen.

photo by Seiko Ogata

ACKNOWLEDGEMENT

I am grateful to the many people who helped me complete this book.
Elizabeth Robin and Alex Yucas: For the sessions with a beautiful marsh view.

The following poems have previously been published.
My gratitude to the editors who chose my pieces for their publications.

Three Shrimp Boats on The Horizon   *Best American Poetry 2023*

Three Shrimp Boats on The Horizon   *WCP Magazine vol. 2 2022*
Hometown
Dead Tide

The Door   *Origami Poems Project (micro chapbook, 2022)*
Full to the Brim
Falling For (Slow)
Weather Forecast (Consequence)
spilled coffee and seeking & finding

Local Honey   *Local Life, May (2022)*

The Door (Unfamiliar Body)   *Music Video with Casey Clark and Andrew K. Clark*
                                            The Hole in The Head Review (2022)

Where The Petals Fall   Nominated for the 2023 Pushcart Prize -
                                            The Petigru Review (2022)

Burnt Ashes   *South Carolina Anthology of BIPOC poets (TBP 2023)*
Burnt Toast

Spring Migration   *Writers.Com (2022)*
                                            Pink (2023)

                                            Lunar Codex (THE POET AND THE
                                            POEM FROM THE LIBRARY OF CONGRESS)

morning glory   *Haiku 2022 (2022) International Haiku Day*
i am fine

The Sea Fog Arrives to Hide the Lies of a Woman Poet (in parts)
                                            Pan Haiku Review (2023)

how you say it   *Tanka America Ribbon (2023)*

Yokohama (The Scale is Confused)   *Soul Spaces Poems on Cities, Towns and Villages*
Helsinki (Approaching Helsinki)   *(Anthology) Authors Press (2023)*

Bird   *Hilton Head Island Poetry Trail #10*
                                            Local Life, October, 2023

TABLE
OF
CONTENTS

The Sea Fog Arrives
to Hide the Lies of a Woman Poet

1.
As I fear for my eyesight you fear our memory.
As you feel for my soul I feel for your mind.

I often visit a walled city in my dreams where the gate
closes at sunset, not a second later or before. With the chart
a wise mathematician's invention, even on a rainy day
the guards with fierce dogs close
the gate promptly at the prescribed time.

I see you just beyond the arch of the gate.

            the field of goldenrods
            where you lost
            your earring

2.
If I dislike making love in darkness, you say, let us
wait for the morning, or even better the afternoon
as the yellow light that comes through the western
window.

> an evening primrose
> standing
> in a rain shower

You fall asleep. Your back is turning red.

> sand dunes
> in the three o'clock
> sun

I go home to drink wine.
I spend the rest of the year in solitude.

3.
I iron your shirt in the winter morning sun.
A large white shirt of cotton. Steam rises.

> first snow
> driving crows run
> for cover

This morning I hear them again.
Red-tailed Hawks near the nest?
Barred Owls going home?
Or is it a funeral?

I wait for the iron to cool
Before putting it away.

> bones
> in an urn

4.
Someone saw me where it couldn't have been me.
A doppelgänger. He was sure. But I know
I was with you on the other
side of the town
at that time on that day.

> without knowing
> plum blossom
> in the late sunset

But it is possible.
My soul lurks elsewhere.
I am not me sometimes.
I might have appeared at the intersection.

> the lips
> in the coldest
> winter afternoon

5.
If you leave me
if I no longer have you in my life
I have thought about that already.

> i went swimming
> toward
> the drop-off

Secretly.
Because I am not supposed to swim alone in the ocean.
The sea fog arrives to hide the lies of the woman poet.

> do you see
> where the whales
> make a turn?

6.
Youth

> summer
> bamboo
> and tree frogs

we left

> freshly
> rinsed grapes in a fine
> meshed colander

behind

> new growth
> in the dirt
> under snow

stays

> one spring
> evening waiting
> with the clock

in my doorway.

7.
What is

        an eggplant,
        grilled, fried, boiled
        or pickled

your

        the eyes
        of a big fat
        catfish

favorite

        popping sesame
        jumping out
        of my old frying pan

food,

        The blossom
        of blackberry gaping
        at my mouth

Mother?

8.

I would like to
love you
for the pleasure of
loving you
and nothing else
in
a town
by
the lake
under
the migrating birds
crossing
the Japan Sea
in the depths
of winter
we arrive
as
twin fishing boats
in
the safe harbor
at
the kitchen window
sparrows
in the sleepy
afternoon
waiting
for
sunset
to bury
red
camellias.

Three Shrimp Boats on The Horizon

Moon.	White.	Seagulls.
Kites.	Cirrus.	Horizon.
Air.	Water.	Wishes.
Turn.	Wait.	Listen.
Shades.	Mirrors.	Distance.
Depth.	Tones.	Whisper.
Prussian.	Blues.	Strings.
Cries.	Lost.	Crystal.
Rock.	Paper.	Scissors.

Full to the Brim

Uprooted marsh grasses
caught in the dock ladder.

The moon, a long-armed puppeteer
making an appearance in the afternoon.

A blade to the sea rides the tide
carrying a dragonfly on its belly.

Bird

After Georges Braque

Before the birds
I was thinking about black holes
or a large cast iron skillet.

I need an oversized
midnight blue egg
for the mural in your Louvre
to give birth to wilder me.

I pull the horizon closer
to catch a seabird.
The boats give a wince.
The crooked current lifts
a gannet with a broken neck.

I let the horizon go.
Winter Solstice crouches
on the starboard side.
And you, you left December.

The Last Swim

For Maggie Schein

How, in a sudden white out, I couldn't tie my hiking boots
and tried again and again, growing angry at you, at me.

How, in winters-ago Wisconsin, a pack of wild wolves
showed a young able-bodied beautiful you the way home.

We talked about disjointed winters perhaps because of
the way the ocean slowly takes our body heat away.

That day, one of the last swimmable autumn days,
we skirted around (no tutus for you) and shivered.

I was conscious of oyster shells, the splinters
on wood planks, hypothermia and your spine.

You wore my fins like new limbs. The sun burnt
my bare back but I was cold in my bones.

King tide forced itself into the intracoastal water.
We stayed in a hollow of a place between the docks.

A poor-postured heron perched by the gangway.
The afternoon was coming to an end.

I look back to see if we left anything behind.
Dry, warm cotton wrapped our salty skin.

The News

In the old swimming pool
through the tinted glass
the water is mildew blue
where there is no true color
all winter and the news
of your departure disregards
the laps. Gradual lightening
of the day follows the fins
stirring the still surface.

A Breath in the Wind

Toes
touch
stir
the sands
swirls
try
to catch
rising
chants
seep
into
my *shakti*
its meaning
left
in the trench
songs
shift keys
shards
repeat
the pause
all is up
the sound
escapes
the gongs
explode
trans—
cend

a breath
in
the wind

the wind.
in
a breath

cend
trans—
explode
the gongs
escapes
the sound
all is up
the pause
repeat
shards
shift keys
songs
in the trench
left
its meaning
my shakti
into
seep
chants
rising
to catch
try
swirls
the sands
stir
touch
Toes

⇑

The Correspondence

Reading the letters between George Sands and Gustave Flaubert

My heart is full
like the ocean
at high tide.

The gentle waves:
I tell you this because
you love me.

I am reading a book
of letters
in the perfect blue.

Till soon, no?
Love from all here,
as ever.

Every time I look up
the sea recedes
from me.

Is this the way to behave?
Almost two months
without writing?

It reveals the sea
floor a question by
a question.

The answer
grows honest
as the tide lowers.

Six Kisses
if you say
yes.

The Difficulties of Open Water Swimming

After Reetika Vazirani

It was more turbulent
than it appeared. But that
was not the only difficulty.

Pelicans glide by
one after another
sometimes low.

She blends in, assimilates
appears as an image
in someone else's success.

Moon straight up.
Eastern horizon deep.
Red of a rose garden.
She discarded garlands.

Change of heart.
Nothing stays still.
The sky abandons every color.

Someone stepped
into the ocean as
she made up her mind.

It's in the genes, we say
as if she is a bag of tricks.
Did she think he was
a trick of light?

Weather Forecast

A little frog is buried
under the hibiscus petals.
By afternoon,
those petals will grow
too large and are
expected to disrupt the sunset.

Hometown

I hear my name
in my mother's voice.
A missing shoe.

Black tulips disappear
into the shadow leaving
white ones behind.

Tofu seller's brass horn.
Tap water cascading.
A baby's cry.

She Likes the First Glimpse

Every night when
the man comes home
he and his wife dress up
in the Period Festival's costumes.

My mother was delusional
pointing at a drab
apartment building
out of her hospital window.

They are so gorgeous
in gold, orange and yellow
only for a little while, then
they turn the lights out.

My mother was talking
to me but
looking through me.
She often did so in her last days.

Where The Petals Fall

落花生 (peanut): the life (生) that begins where the petals (花) fall (落)

Flower

Peanut blossoms
pollinate themselves
early in the morning
and fall.

Seeds will grow
underground, underneath
where the flower
perishes
knowing
the daughter
will never
know her mother.

Mother

Half an orphan, in bed.
I never knew my mother's mother
who sang and laughed.

Sitting at the desk,
I read "Being a Flower"
late at night.

No other way of being
but be a flower
The flower pushes back
without losing its shape [1]

---

1 Ishihara Yoshiro, *Being a Flower,* translated by Miho Kinnas

Daughter

Mother no longer leaves the futon.

Today, my son came home
monsters in his head.

I clean the floorboard on my hands and knees.

Yokohama

I am drawing a map
to my parents' house on the hill.
The scale is confused.
There are many inaccuracies.

A little corner fruit shop is now a pet store.
Time may be psychological.
My boyfriend was always late.

Older taxi drivers know the tomb-stone cutter.
Young ones know it like a ghost story.
The road zips through the fire station.

The big chestnut tree
no longer there where all summer
cicadas spent their one week on earth.

They were so loud —we often gave up talking, listened
to them rolling our eyes to each other and broke into a big laughter.
That shut them up!

One day coming home from school a concrete pole blocked
our view of the hill. My mother complained to the electric company.
It is still there.

A boy threw a pebble at my window. I was on the phone
with another boy. I draw a little heart.
All three hearts were broken.

My mother served bowls of ramen noodle for my friends
complete with pork, eggs, sesame seeds, scallions
seaweed and spinach.

My mother began taking rests
on the way up the hill
the way my father did in his late years.

The day I saw my mother for the last time
she staggered out of the house without a cane.
I am fine, I am fine, don't worry, I'm fine. I draw a stick figure.

With her open sky smile she held onto the edge of the fence with her right hand, her left hand sparkled a little. I draw her waving hand.
She watched my brother drive me away.

The Pitch

Five mornings in a row, my mother tells me about her dreams.
She keeps dreaming about her childhood in Manchuria.

> *Like the silhouette on the revolving lantern.*
> *Kaleidoscopic.*
> *The sun was stunning dipping into the horizon!*
> *How thick the ice was on the lake in the forest!*
> *Did I tell you about the stolen skates we found*
> *at the thieves' market in the morning?*

In one of the last dreams I heard
she was a thirteen-year-old entrepreneur.
She and her friends sold cigarettes to passersby
near the Harbin bridge.

> *Our sales pitch was in Chinese and Russian!*
> *Choyan ma? Su-kirt?*
> *Choyan ma? Su-kirt?*

> *I may die soon.*
> *If you leave now I won't see you again.*

I didn't believe her.
I still hear her voice repeating the pitch
with a chuckle in between.

Earthquake

Earthquakes have
a way of shaking only the air
not the house with the door that
needs a little lift to lock or unlock.

Trying to Date a Family Photo

My family has been a parishioner of the temple for centuries.
The corners of old tombstones are rounded.
The hem of my father's winter coat touches the edge of the chamber.
It's cloudy. Mt. Fuji is invisible.
Our favorite eel restaurant closes on Mondays.
My father's shirt collar is too loose. His tie is black.
It's a memorial: Grandfather's 17th or Grandmother's 33rd.
My cousin's dress is blue.
My aunt is wheel-chair bound.
My brother has lost weight.
My mother hides behind the sunglasses, ageless.
The school-photo smile of my daughter looks twelve.
My father is to be gone within three years.

A Woman with the Head of a Peony

after a wood sculpture by Asanoi Haruna

She brought home a sculpture, thirty centimeters tall
made of wood, a woman
with the head of a peony.

The woman looks above the horizon.
Her skinny legs and arms follow gravity.
Her head is a cloud.

She carries a red handbag with nothing in it.
She has no use for lipstick or a comb.
Crumpled tissue paper sits on her shoulders.

The daughter left her father twice
both times with not
with a Kate Spade but a suitcase.

She stands on a block
the last square of the carved life.
A faceless woman.

Did she hear
his unspoken unconditional
in the back of her head?

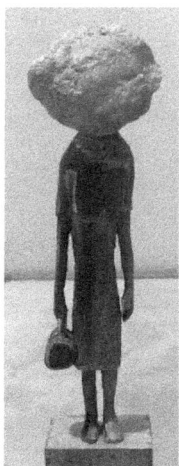

Sculpture by Asanoi Haruna
Photo by Kyoko Ono

Spirit

With a huge freezer, a widow
moves into an apartment. To open
she transfers the bowls and plates
off the freezer. To find
the lemon cake her husband loved.
A bag of peas burns her fingertips.
After closing the lid, she moves
the plates and bowls back.

Barn Burning

A map of burnt barns
found in the bottom drawer.
Did you know the stories?
Whether it was a father or
a pretty girlfriend, he thought he
had a role.
But he didn't.

From The Lying Life of Adults
by Elena Ferrante

"Where did you go?"
"To Uncle Nicola's house, he says hello to you."
"How did he seem to you?"
"A little dumb."

Unsolved mysteries.
a rational mind would say
unsolved is redundant.
What about
pointless miracles?

Completely common names.
Ichiro went by his first name
because Suzuki Ichiro was just like
Yamada Hanako or Jane Smith.
Too common to be true.

If freeing banal words
to manifest unexpected energy
is poetry, then
poetry is protest.
Then is poetry political?

Excerpt

After Cathy Park Hong,
Excerpt from the Historian's Memoir (Dance Dance Revolution)

At the airport
where
our layover
continued
his mind was soaring
like a birdcage.

The illustrator
of smaller things
etched a spigot
on an old sink
and it immediately
squirted a bird.

The canary of
spiral blue
dropped a puzzle
in the corner of
a city.

He sighed
three times a day
fell asleep
for four minutes
at a time.

Day-dreams
a draft of smoke
took off
beyond
the rusted horizon.

A shot.

Reading Henri Cole

The Blue Heron
looked up at the sky.

So did
I.

We watched an Osprey
circle.

Henri Cole
had to wait.

Haiku and Tanka

a frog jumps
after burning ashes
they are no fireflies

I won't tell you
about turmeric tea
building my stockpile

burnt bacon
for a few seconds
the dog forgets me

I was looking for you
In a bag of groceries
on the table
burnt toast's smell
lingering

dancing in the morning sun
spilled ground coffee
single origin: Columbia

I am fine
until crisp iceberg lettuce
brings out my tears

standing
next to a stranger
at the fireworks
I feel honest —
a green skirt

how long have
the children been
seeking & finding?

I walk a dog
(should be in the past tense)
I walk alone

I walk between two
pine trees; I wish
they weren't so straight

In the darkness
of your heart, I write
to you about the things
that make my heart
beat faster

stealing dreams
my arm eases
under your pillow

my shadow skips ahead
I still can't catch up with you —
the spring equinox

it wasn't your fault
dark tulips swung
a little too hard

turning a page
an ant falls
on the word —
I like how you
say it, 'love'

Tokyo harbor
never sleep
august moon
wanes
counterclockwise

The Work of Art

1. For My Sisters[2]

On the wall of an old factory turned into a studio
a painter draws a village. Bucolic, peaceful, traditional.
A good Chinese village before the famine.

Farmhouses, a couple sitting on the bench by the bridge.
Girls laughing, singing, washing, and cooking.
I created a beautiful ladies' kingdom. A grand view garden.

Come closer to the painting.
The women are vivacious and beautiful.
We notice some bubbles in the painting.

The black-booted painter walks away.
Bubbles are rising; Bubbles are everywhere.
I wrote the story consciously; I wrote consciously for women.

It is an underwater village.
The village sank into the dam on the night of the wedding.
The garden in the deep woods of peach trees, drenched.

Where no one from the outside has ever entered.
I wrote the story consciously.
Women are vivacious and beautiful.

Girls are in a natural state.
Women and girls before they get married.
I love them.

---

2 An Interview with Wang Anyi, *Feminism with Chinese Characteristics.*

2. The Analects for Women

adhering barren concubine
duty eyes filial
guilty husband intolerable
jealousy kinsman labyrinthine
must never only
perform question repress
submission total unobtrusive
virtuous wrong extortion
yielding zealous Analects

3. To My Sisters[3]

Clothes hanging out on the cluttered bamboo poles
hint at private lives.
Like the opening scenes of a good movie, we immerse
ourselves in the alley.
In the garden, potted balsams, ghost flowers,
scallions and garlic are breathing.
We tend them, tend our elders, spouses
children and the sick.
With western dress sizes on their lips
they are thinking about the fabric for their next chongsam.

Because she let the fate take her
he dutifully gave her a ride.

Broken roof tiles laid in disarray.
I move to new houses same curtains, large flowers.
The pigeon cage on the roof is empty.
If only we could see the city like those pigeons.
How much is friendship worth?
Is it *a little plant floating,*
lotus in murky water or
a large fish circumscribing?

Is it worth just as much for a woman as the world?

The morning is new and fresh
but not without a past
in the city called Shanghai.

---

3   After *The Song of Ever Lasting Sorrow: A Novel of Shanghai* by Wang Anyi

4. Opium in The House[4]

There's no
history in China;
today has it all.

Fattened
woman buried
in cushions.

Swallow two tiny
pieces of opium
with brandy.

Why do we
live
only once?

Jade Peach.
The grandfather's
concubine.

A secret
will bury
the truth.

She must
have been truly
in love with him.

I am sure
it was
money.

The hidden
truth will bury
other truths.

How do you think
she died?
Speculate that!

---

4 After the Japanese Translation of Lynn Pan's *Tracing it Home*

(English translation by Miho Kinnas)

5. Deliberation

Women gather
around a pile of potatoes
elbowing the competition.
They grab a potato, examine it
through glasses, above their glasses
Weigh them in trained hands and put them
back in the pile, shaking their heads. Pick another
and another, as if finding a bride for the eldest son.

6. Running Away from the Doll House

After the May Fourth movement
she wanted to learn to read and write
but grandmother and mother bound her feet.
After losing the son she left for Peking
met other new women and wrote free verse.
Having heard about a marriage based on love
she wrote a public letter and ended her arrangement.
She joined the Republic's feminist movement.
Arrested by the communists for publishing
a radical magazine, she was then hanged.

7. Expat's Living Room

tiny lotus shoes
decorate the coffee table
not salt and pepper

8. Match Box

I didn't think of feminism, I simply saw reality. Wang Anyi, *Am I a Feminist?*

Trying to remember the name of the movie
the bus driver writes a love poem for his self-absorbed wife
from a match box. I now want to study a match box, but I cannot find one.
In my head, I conjure up a match box I saw in the Café Art Deco.

Pictured is a hula girl and a palm tree against the tropical sky.
I don't remember the name of the manufacturer.
It rests on a table by a famous designer with a chrome base.
I ask the waitress with a deep slit in a tight dress, but she doesn't know.

I see a girl's face and the side of the match.
What's the name of the side used to strike the match head?
Enough with not knowing the names.

I lose names.

It is no longer a match box.
It is just a keepsake.

I am certain that the keepsake has six surfaces, even though I only see two.
Half of it is hidden behind a silver ice bucket.
The half of the girl's head is hidden behind the tong.
I suspect the girl is wholesome.

I reach out and pick up the keepsake.
It feels weightless in my palms.
I shake it.
It sounds
I*sts, ists* and i*sms, isms*.
I don't know how they got there.
I will handle the collectibles with caution.

9. Outside Old Shanghai

Scrap metal
is not a metaphor, a man pedals
the bicycle that pulls the heap
that sinks the wagon, followed
by a woman pushing the burden as if
holding up the wrongs of the city.
Averted glances meet
the distant neon tubes, drip the horizon
in the rear-view mirror.
The black van honks
glaring the steady rain.
A charming girlfriend of yours mumbles
in a playful tone,
"That's a hard life."

10. Piano

A nameless upright
filled the tiny room
yellowed keys too slack
to keep up with the barking dog.
Someone left patriotic sheet music on the stand.
The sun from the tiny window seized the flag.

11. Yokohama, 1973

The eyes of red guards are shining brightly.
That was all we knew about them.

Slender, tall swimmers came from Shanghai.
When clothed it was hard to tell girls from boys.

Their girls stood like Cedars —our girls taught
to "perch" not "sit,' and not to obstruct others' view.

Our girls prepared frozen lemon slices covered in a lot
of sugar for every competition. Their girls didn't.

All the competitors bow to the swimming pool
when they leave the lane after the race.

Their eyes are shining brightly in the summer sun.
Do you think they are the Red Guards at home?

12. Elegant Things[5]

After The Pillow book 29

A white cover coat worn over a violet waistcoat.
Pulled silk whispers.
Unfamiliar bird calls from the top of a birch.

Duck eggs.
Drop a surprise.
Listening.

Liana syrup over shaved ice in a shiny silver bowl.
Your reflection, escaping
the last spoonful.

A rosary - rock crystal.
Holds you still.
Am I at the right place?

Wisteria blossoms.
Follow the undulation.
Clouds will break open.

Plum blossoms in snow.
Your last thought without a word
dark red the last flame.

A child eating strawberries.

---

[5] *The Pillow Book* is a Zuihitsu, a creative non-fiction, written by Sei Shonagon of 11th century Japan. By this time, Japanese literature was well established: however, the Chinese culture was still regarded as more learned and sophisticated. Women writers like Sei Shonagon and Murasaki Shikibu (the author of *The Tale of Genji*) shed Chinese influence ahead of their male counterparts and wrote them in a freer, elegant prose style.

The poems 12 *Elegant Things* and 13 *Flute* express the impression that The Pillow Book is elegant, dreamy, and feminine. However, the tragic reality that Empress Consort Teishi, the protagonist of *The Pillow Book,* faced because of her gender in the patriarchal society is often forgotten. The author, also being female, adds the overly biased association of *The Pillow Book* with female sexuality. Poem 14, *The Pillow Book,* tells the behind-the-scenes story of why and how Sei Shonagon wrote *The Pillow Book.*

I was the child eating strawberries.
We cannot return, we cannot give up.

13. Flute

After The Pillow Book 205

You hear it.

Flute heard from afar
coming closer a little by little.

You are my Empress.
Flute heard next door
leaving us into the night.

I am in-waiting forever.

Imagine a flute carried
everywhere in his sleeve.

I find one by the bed.
I know your danger.
I wrap it in paper when sent for.

Like a pristine letter.

Your memory of happiness.

Flute heard in the middle of the night.
Your Emperor plays it for you.

Only for you.

It is most exquisite.

14. The Pillow Book

Sei Shonagon brushed me
on the pages of valuable white paper
gifted by the empress
stacked as high as a pillow.

The empress who found love
in political marriage
one in thousands, tens of thousands
but she was falling.

I was born in the dark time in her despair.
One wish Sei Shonagon made
that I, the book, would provide solace
to the empress.

Every phrase and word considered carefully
for my survival.
People say I am full of dreamy ideas and whims
spurred by moments in the daily life of Sei Shonagon.

She filled me with snow, colored leaves, wisterias, and warblers.
Babies, festivals, ceremonies. The pompous aristocratic man snuck
into a wrong room. Full of love affairs, gossips, poetry, and scent.

My author was one of the ladies-in-waiting
who embodied the will and wishes of the empress
the mastermind of the salon.
There is no point repeating tragedies in writing.

The salon was filled with the lines from the Chinese classics
and Kokinshu poems.
Wits and jokes.
Laughter and music.

The empress died in childbirth.
The baby prince, the last thing
the enemies wanted.
I am given the task of telling the tales

of the powerful enemies.
I must survive the period of their influence.

Helsinki

The engine hummed all night
like a 3-D printer
building the city.

In the darkest hour
of the white night
the ship jerked once.

Men in blue and yellow
uniforms hooked
the anchoring ropes.

On the pier a few workers
dragged the covered cargo
on wheels slowly across.

The container trucks
that had gone first
in Stockholm filed out.

The ferry continues
the Baltic voyage
the thick fog is lifting.

Seagulls reappear
in the leftover sunrise
suddenly.

The maritime fortress
built in the eighteenth-century
Suomenlinna

punctuates the history
obscures the earlier times
and reminds of the present war.

Nearing the harbor
more gulls circle.
I approach Helsinki from the sea.

Wildflowers

Northern Ireland

From the stone pier
young men jump
feet first
into the Irish Sea
white skin turning pink.
They weren't around when
the crescent moon rose in red.

Mackerels jump
beyond the outer jetty.
The clouds
wispy and broken.
Wind directions shift.
Scales reflect the weak sun.
An old weather saying:
They make tall ships carry low sails.

Bouquets of wildflowers
protect boundaries
from evil fairies.
Bright yellow ones are marsh marigold.
Pale ones primrose.
However, says ancient folklore:
the night scent of buttercup
may cause madness.

Two girls on the pavement
along the shuttered shops
learn to roller-skate
and not to hate
but to ask, why.

Bridal

After Lola Ridge / For Leslie

Deer drinking
from a stream
The sound of twigs

Losing the thought
of a forgotten name
in mid-sentence

Clouds
at eye-level
The Pinnacle Rock

The wind is
The new-washed
hand

Dogs run through
the song-lines
between a star and a cricket

At night, the sound
of stealthy animal brushes
the night woods

It comes down
to chiffon or organza
Your wedding dress

Diorama of Rice

It became a full moon
We couldn't cut aluminum foil
into a crescent

The imposter moon
covered with your sticky
fingerprints

Diorama of rice
told a thousand and one
veiled stories

Grains of rice
placed on a shell excavated
from the mountain

We made a
special wool rug
from an old slipper

Scorpions
hid under
a wall of carpets

We slept
like mother and daughter
in the Arabian desert

Paint dried
in the morning and you
held it like a crown

The key chains
on your backpack
didn't jingle

Local Honey

Drenched in gentle
rain, sinking into soft mud, soaked
in the spring sun. You know how
nice things in life can be messy
and tangled. Drizzle and plunge.
Slathered, spilled
over, your fingers
golden.

Spring Migration

After the blood test we drive downtown.
Turning down Liberty, we wait
for the pedestrians to cross.
Above, birds flutter from palmetto
to palmetto pecking fermenting fruits.

The sky cerulean blue.
Cedar waxwings keep passing fruit.
As if being chased by a big shadow
they take no chances.
They are chased by life in the air, but sometimes
every bird in the flock finds a spot

on the branches of a large gum tree.
A bare tree.
Their constant buzzing calls cease.
Facing north-east they stay still.   Still.
How much longer? I count my heartbeats.

The tree is too tall for me to catch their colors
Shifting in my seat, I see with my mind's eye
the dashing black around the head
blondish crest, yellow hemmed tail
the red droplets on their wings, melted wax.

Each body, one ounce of divination
swinging through the spring sunlight
tomorrow, after tomorrow, another tomorrow.
I turn to you, on top of the wheel
the sun on your knuckles.

The Etymology of Species

Deep in the forest
Karakuri, the wooden contraption,
turned and turned.

Birds with a long tail
emerged first
in the east wind.

A giant owl towered
the center tree and stayed still
Nobody knew it was dead.

The body dangled by the third night
and became a symbol
for a head on a pike.

> Hawks kept hunting

> Ducks stayed monogamous

> Pigeons went on cooing.

> Sparrows are feeding.

Before long, villagers
set a net and began trapping
every newborn bird.

Birds became
the thing to be caught.
Karakuri stopped turning.

The villagers used the parts for fire.

The Images from Mars

After Craig Arnold

A young poet went missing
inside the crater
Japanese archipelago.

The volcano has erupted twice
since.
Seismic activities are picking up.

> *each year harder to live within*
> *each year harder to live without*

In the images from Mars
ash-covered hills and plains
are somehow familiar

like the great-grandchild
I'll never meet.

December Egg

With each rain, the winter deepens.
The last egg in a soggy carton.

You will be scrambled in the morning.
You won't lead the free-ranged life.

I heard about dinosaures living as birds.
You might be the missing link.

You may grow teeth instead of wings.

I will never know because you will be
cracked, stirred and fried.

I wish you'd message me
you could blink blue or start rolling.

It's past midnight.
What do you say?

Opportunity

An Ethiopian cheesemaker immigrated to Italy
herding fifteen goats.
She grew her business and hired refugees.

She was killed
by a Ghanian migrant, her body
found trampled by the flock.

Aunty West owned a bar.
An employee swung a baseball bat
at her head over a small loan.

A Singing Stone

The first time I heard the stone
it was dark.

I turned the light on
it went quiet.

The stone on the kitchen counter
one of the plethora of things

my son keeps bringing home. Today
he returned salty from the beach

with a pink dotted shell
and I heard it clearly:

I wish I had been your lover or mother.

My son, with keener hearing
didn't seem to notice.

Instead, he said I must be bothered
by something

because I turned the water on a bit
too hard

and it was splashing the sink edge. But he
didn't mention the sound I made

dicing a piece of ham:
much louder and larger than usual.

These days I hear it more often.
The voice is becoming familiar.

Thursday

4 am   A dream woke me: The baby fell into a hole,
and I didn't follow to rescue her.

5 am   In German, "boredom" is "a long while";
in Buddhism, "mental defeat".

6 am   Watching a shrimp boat offshore,
a melody from *Carnaval* began playing.

7 am   A brown dog hugged me on the beach,
and my hand still smells of dog.

8 am   A paper crane adds the smell of a cinnamon bun to my fingers.

9 am   *Pierrot* and *Harlequin*: the one with the wand is not *Pierrot*.

10 am   Fish jumps; Paganini's Caprice is Take Five.

11 am   The husband and wife think the same thoughts,
in different orders.

noon   YouTube archives:
Horowitz played *Carnaval* with many wrong notes.

1 pm   Too much cream drowns his schnitzel.

2 pm   *1976*, compound sentences clatter Jackie Kay's biography.

3 pm   The craving for an ingredient like salt and vinegar
is hard to appease.

4 pm   Continuation; Found poem my own:
"You miss me so much. I must be lost."

5 pm   The heart was made of waxed napkins, like a rose.

Happiness Pancake

I have the bowls ready
for flour, baking powder, a pinch of salt.
You separate yolk and white.
Three eggs.
We whip
from semi-transparency
to shaping into snow white.
Stir in sugar
four separate times.

No rushing —

I combine
yolk, milk and flour mix.
You fold egg white.
Keep the bubbles intact.
I add a splash of vanilla essence.
The colors merge.

Gradually—

You heat the skillet
make it hot
drop and spread butter.
I place the skillet
on a wet cloth.
When the temperature is
just right we
pour the dough.

Sizzles—

The happiest fragrance
in the world
fills the house.
Pancake is browning.
Pancake is rising.

A little secret—

Have the lid ready

and add a bit of water.
Let the pancake steam
just a little while longer.

For You

I've misplaced a card
chosen for you
from the rack of pinks and reds.
Who shall I be for you?
Having finally found the one
I made sure cats wouldn't scratch it;
goldfish couldn't sprinkle it.
But like I said: I cannot find it.
I've searched everywhere
between the messages, behind
the closet doors, under the pillows.
I hear you saying:
You must have misplaced me long ago
in your previous life.

The East Exit

Red amaryllis
on the side of the road
without a leaf.

The sixth floor
not too high
not too soon.

They are not
my hands shading
the setting sun.

Still, I see you
by the East exit.
I wasn't there.

The Door

A door just opened on a street.
A love affair that lasted a lifetime
stepped onto the pavement.

I was held in such a familiar way
while learning the unfamiliar body.
We had all the time in the world, as if.

A love affair that lasted a lifetime
didn't look back at the closing door
of the bus I had missed.

Arpeggio

Listening to *Contemplation*

Warming
hands around
my coffee cup
it is the last day of May
winter never leaves
summer without you
pauses the time
seeping through
thick layers
of water
above
gathering the broken
arpeggio
groping
for you.

Where Did You Learn to Dress Like That?

I am a daughter
of a wealthy Persian merchant
in the Tang dynasty Xian.

I am his souvenir.

Many court me with treasures:
A dragon's heart
bamboos of five colors
or a jade-clustered comb.

I am a festival

in the walled city of the maze.
I might tell you about the place
but not how to get there.

Falling For

a camellia
an ant crawls
on fingers

fungus
grows like ears
under leaves

an afternoon quiet
fingertips
barely touch

nude
tiny
at the edge of resolve

my knees
in the hot springs
laughing

Once

I won't
link you to what
I'll miss.

I saw a message
my swift pulse
flashing: "Bliss!"

Light changes.
I will let
someone else fill it.

That night
an umbrella fell
from the bodies.

Your jackets
tobacco smell
a touch.

This is the End of a Line

A piece of string
two fingers tight
around the invisible.

The delicate, luminous texture
made from silk moths.
Moths will not fly or eat.

kiss me, re-kiss me & kiss me again[6]

Did the beautiful rope-maker
write it?

The fraying ends
of the piece of thread
        begin the ideogram

for apparition, phantom, ghost
        shadow, or illusion
but the best translation for it is "a trick."

---

6 From a sonnet of Louise Labé (c. 1520-1566).
   She was also known as the Beautiful Rope maker.

About the Author

Twice nominated for the Pushcart Prize, Miho Kinnas is a translator, writer, and poet. This book is her third poetry collection following *Today, Fish Only* and *Move Over, Bird*, both by Math Paper Press. The poem, *Three Shrimp Boats on The Horizon*, was selected for Best American Poetry 2023. Also in 2023, a book of collaborated poetry with E. Ethelbert Miller, *We Eclipse into the Other Side*, was published by Pinyon Publishing. In addition, a rengay written with Lenard D. Moore appeared in Tandem, Vol2, No2 and her translation in Tokyo Poetry Journal Vol 12. She writes literary essays and book reviews for journals including E-Markings, American Book Review and Literary Shanghai Alluvium. Her interview and reading recorded on Grace Cavalieri's radio/podcast show *The Poem and the Poet* will be heading for permanent installation on the moon later in the year. She holds MFA in creative writing from the City University of Hong Kong.

She is an instructor at Writers.com, Camp Conroy, New York Writers' Workshop and Life-Long Learning of Hilton Head. She offers poetry workshops based on Japanese short poetic forms.

Contact: miho.kinnas@gmail.com

www.ingramcontent.com/pod-product-compliance
Lightning Source LLC
Chambersburg PA
CBHW070124100426
42744CB00010B/1915